不同的文化

Social Emotional and Multicultural Learning |
Non-Fiction Series

Copyright © 2022 by Level Learning, INC. and Washington Yu Ying PCS™
Original and Edited Text Copyright © 2022 by Washington Yu Ying PCS™

All rights reserved. No part of this book in whole or part may be reproduced without written permission from the publisher.

Published by Level Learning, INC.

Content Contributors:
Washington Yu Ying PCS™
Level Learning - Ya-Ching Chang

Illustrations by: Matt Austin

Leveling classification based on Level Learning standard. For full description, visit www.levellearning.com

ISBN 978-1-64040-083-2
Simplified Chinese Edition

About Level Learning:
Level Learning provides a literacy focused curriculum specifically designed for K-12 Chinese as a Second Language classrooms. Our program offers 20 levels of specific and detailed objectives, leveled texts and passages, mastery-based online assessment, and analytics to enable data-driven instruction. Level Learning reading curriculum for both literature and informational text emphasize grammar and comprehension skills to help teachers develop confident and independent Chinese language readers. The non-fiction series of books are specifically designed to support our informational text course based on multiple national standards. To learn more about our entire offering, visit www.levellearning.com.

About Washington Yu Ying PCS™:
Washington Yu Ying PCS is a Mandarin English dual language immersion International Baccalaureate (IB) World school. Yu Ying's mission is to inspire and prepare young people to create a better world by challenging them to reach their full potential in a nurturing Chinese/English educational environment. Yu Ying's comprehensive IB, dual immersion curriculum equips students with global competencies for success in the real world. As a leader in immersion education, Yu Ying is determined to advance Chinese language programs and global citizenry education by helping other schools create and strengthen their Chinese programs. For more information, email: products@washingtonyuying.org

美国，有许多来自世界各地的移民。这些来自不同国家的人，带来了不同的文化。

有时候，我们可能听不懂他们说的话。有时候，我们可能不理解他们的行为。有时候，我们可能因为不了解他们的文化，而产生误会。

比如说，中国移民认为做人谦虚很重要。当别人夸奖他们的时候，他们通常会说自己还不够好。

但是在美国,有自信是非常重要的。他们会很开心地接受别人的夸奖。

中国移民认为说话要和气。他们有时候害怕伤人,不会直接说出自己的想法。他们喜欢客气地说出自己的看法。

但是在美国,表达自己的想法很重要。人们会直接说出自己的感觉或看法。

中国移民认为尊敬长辈很重要。年轻人要听长辈的话，要对长辈有礼貌。

但是在美国,不管年纪大小,都可以像朋友一样相处。年轻人可以直接叫长辈的名字。

因为不同的文化背景，人们会有不同的看法或行为。了解不同的文化，可以帮助我们互相尊重，减少误会。

Glossary

	Pinyin	English Definition
各地	gè dì	various places
移民	yí mín	immigrants
不同	bù tóng	different
文化	wén huà	culture
懂	dǒng	to comprehend, to understand
理解	lǐ jiě	to understand
行为	xíng wéi	behavior
了解	liǎo jiě	to realize, to find out
产生	chǎn shēng	to produce
误会	wù huì	misunderstanding
比如说	bǐ rú shuō	for example
认为	rèn wéi	to believe
谦虚	qiān xū	modest
重要	zhòng yào	important
夸奖	kuā jiǎng	to praise

	Pinyin	English Definition
够	gòu	enough
自信	zì xìn	self-confidence
接受	jiē shòu	to accept
和气	hé qi	friendly, polite
害怕	hài pà	afraid
伤	shāng	to hurt
直接	zhí jiē	direct
想法	xiǎng fǎ	way of thinking
客气	kè qi	polite
看法	kàn fǎ	opinion
表达	biǎo dá	to express
感觉	gǎn jué	feeling
尊敬	zūn jìng	to respect
长辈	zhǎng bèi	elder
年轻	nián qīng	young

Glossary

	Pinyin	English Definition
礼貌	lǐ mào	courteous, politeness
不管	bù guǎn	regardless
背景	bèi jǐng	background
尊重	zūn zhòng	respect
减少	jiǎn shǎo	to reduce

www.ingramcontent.com/pod-product-compliance
Lightning Source LLC
Chambersburg PA
CBHW041221070526
44584CB00001B/39